THE SUN

our nearest star

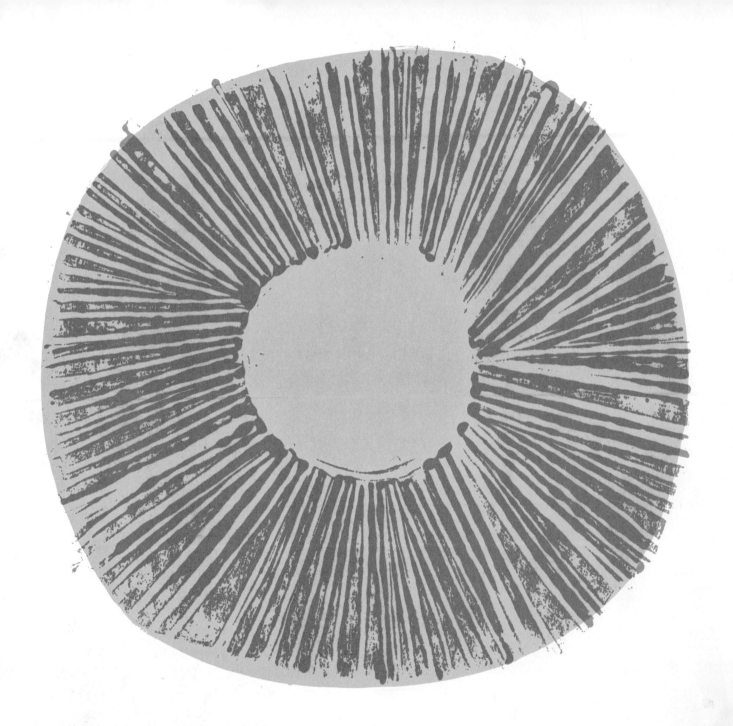

FRANKLYN M. BRANLEY

THE SUN
our nearest star

pictures by HELEN BORTEN

Thomas Y. Crowell Company · New York

REC® LIBRARY EDITION

LET'S-READ-AND-FIND-OUT SCIENCE BOOKS

Editors: *DR. ROMA GANS,* Professor Emeritus of Childhood Education, Teachers College, Columbia University

DR. FRANKLYN M. BRANLEY, Chairman of The American Museum—Hayden Planetarium, consultant on science in elementary education

*AVAILABLE IN SPANISH

REC Library Edition reprinted with the permission of Thomas Y. Crowell Company

Responsive Environments Corp., Englewood Cliffs, N. J. 07632

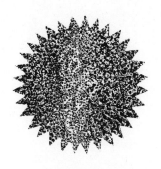

*the sun
our
nearest
star*

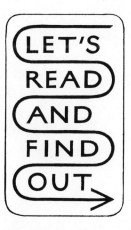

You see stars at night.
In the daytime you do not see stars.
But there is a star in the daytime sky.
It is the star nearest to earth.
It is the star nearest to you.
We do not call it a star.
We call it the sun.

Yes, the sun is a star.
The sun is our only daytime star.

The sun is big.
How big do you think it is:
    as big as a car,
    as big as a house,
    as big as a train?

The sun is bigger; much, much bigger.

5

Do you think the sun is as big as a big boat?

It is bigger; much, much bigger.

Do you think the sun is as big as a whole town?

The sun is bigger. It is much, much bigger.

The sun is bigger than a train, or a boat, or a whole
   town.
The sun is bigger than the moon.
The sun is bigger than the earth.
It is much, much bigger.

11

If the earth were this big,

the sun would be this big.
The sun is very, very big.

The sun is far away.

The moon is far away, but the sun is much farther away.

Suppose a car could go to the moon.

A fast car would take six months to reach the moon.

Suppose the car could go to the sun.

The car would take 200 years to reach the sun.

Six months to the moon—200 years to the sun.

The sun is far away. It is very, very far to the sun.

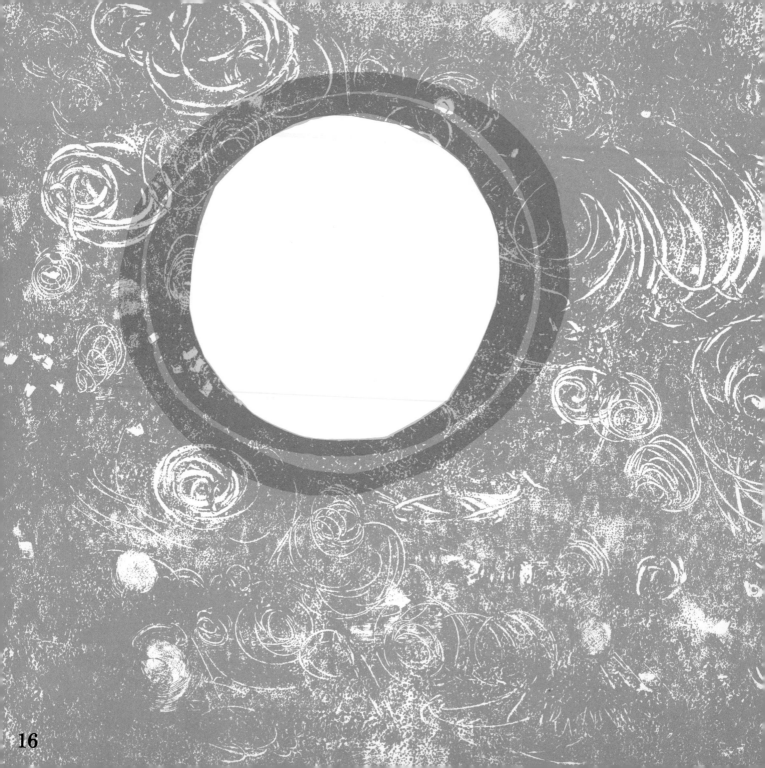

The sun is a sphere.
A sphere is like a ball.
A sphere is round all around.
The sun is big.
The sun is far away.
The sun is a sphere.

The sun is very, very, very hot.

A match flame is hot. The sun is much hotter than a match flame.

A stove gets hot. The sun is much hotter than a hot stove.

A light bulb gets hot. The sun is much hotter than a hot light bulb.

The sun is much, much hotter than anything on earth.

The sun helps us.

The sun makes daisies grow.

The sun makes corn grow.

The sun makes all plants grow.

Try this experiment. The experiment will show you
that the sun makes plants grow.

Get two tin cans.
Put soil in each can.
Plant six bean seeds in each can.
Put one can in the sun.
Put one can in a dark place.
Put some water on the soil in each can.
The soil should be kept damp, but not wet.

Watch the beans. After eight or ten days they will start to grow.

The beans in the sun grow well.

The beans in the dark grow well.

Leave the cans in the same places. Do not move them.

Leave one can in the sun.

Leave one can in the dark.

Leave them there for many days.

Leave them there for three weeks, if you can.

25

Water the beans a little bit each day.
Water them only enough to keep the soil damp, not
  wet.
Do the beans in the dark grow?
Do the beans in the sun grow?
Which beans grow better?

Beans need the sun.

All plants need the sun.

Everything that is alive needs the sun.

You are alive. You need the sun.

Your dog is alive. He needs the sun.

We all need the sun.

Suppose there were no sun in the sky.
There would be no flowers.
There would be no beans.
There would be no you. There would be no dog.
There would be no plants or animals.

Now you know that:

There is a star in the daytime sky.

The sun is the star of the daytime.

It is a sphere.

It is far away.

It gives us light.

It keeps us warm.

You need the sun.

We all need the sun.

ABOUT THE AUTHOR

FRANKLYN M. BRANLEY is Assistant Chairman and Astronomer at the American Museum-Hayden Planetarium where he has contact with audiences of all ages and where he directs the diverse educational program. For many years he has helped children learn scientific facts and principles at an early age without impairing their sense of wonder about the world they live in. Before coming to the Planetarium, Dr. Branley taught science at many grade levels including the lower elementary grades, high school, college, and graduate school.

Dr. Branley received his training for teaching at the State University of New York at New Paltz, at New York University, and Columbia University. He lives with his wife and two daughters in Woodcliff Lake, New Jersey.

ABOUT THE ARTIST

HELEN BORTEN has illustrated several books for children and is the author and illustrator of two others: *Do You See What I See?* and *Do You Hear What I Hear?*

Mrs. Borten was born in Philadelphia, Pennsylvania, and was graduated from the Philadelphia Museum College of Art. She lives with her husband and two sons, Peter and Laurence, in Lafayette Hill, Pennsylvania.